TAKE UP YOUR CROSS

Lenten Bible Stories for Kids

JARED DEES

For more information visit jareddees.com.

Paperback: ISBN 978-1-954135-02-4
eBook: ISBN 978-1-954135-03-1

First Edition

CONTENTS

AN INTRODUCTION FOR PARENTS AND TEACHERS

The Bible stories in this collection are meant to help kids develop a deeper relationship with God the Father and the Son he sent to die for us, Jesus Christ. The season of Lent is a forty-day journey with Jesus to his death and resurrection on Easter. It is a time of prayer, self-sacrifice, and thinking of others.

In this collection, you will find stories from the Old Testament that show the significance of the number forty. There are parables to teach about the three pillars of Lent: prayer, fasting, and almsgiving. Most of all, though, you will find short stories about the events leading up to and including Jesus Christ's death on the cross.

The stories in this collection will teach kids important lessons about these concepts:

- Temptation & Sin

- Prayer
- Self-Sacrifice
- Forgiveness
- Gratitude

Each of the stories in the collection is very short. They are probably shorter than most bedtime stories for younger kids. They are short because even a brief break of time with the Bible can have an enormous effect on you and your children.

You should be able to read each story in just a few minutes. The discussions that you have with your kids might be short, too, or you may find yourselves talking for a long time about the questions that the stories bring up.

The reflection questions for each story are meant to get kids to remember what they read but also reflect on how it relates to their lives. Help them understand what happened in each Bible story, but go further and get them to see what God wants them to think about personally as they read.

I am so pleased that you have decided to invite children to experience these stories with you. The best thing about Bible stories is that each time we read them, we experience God speaking to us in new ways. Whether you or your kids are reading these stories again or for the first time, open up your hearts to God and see what he wants to reveal to you as you reflect on these words.

AN INTRODUCTION FOR CHILDREN

I have a secret for you. Parents don't like punishing their kids.

It's true. I know, because I am a dad. Although I get angry from time to time and even yell at my children, I don't like being angry with them. I don't like punishing them. I don't like yelling. I don't like sending my kids to their rooms. I don't like taking away dessert after dinner or giving them extra chores.

But sometimes punishment is important. Kids are less likely to cheat on a test if they know they will be kicked out of school. When a teenager is grounded for staying out too late, they are probably going to think twice about missing curfew again.

I have another secret for you. God doesn't like punishing his kids either. He doesn't like punishing his people for their sins, but throughout history, people have continued to disobey God and turn away from him again and again.

There are always consequences for our actions. When we turn away from God's help, life gets worse. When we try to do things alone, we are more likely to fail. We all sin—every one of us. But does God give up on us? No. He sent his only Son to help us.

God sent his beloved Son, Jesus, to suffer and die. It was a punishment for a sin he didn't commit. He was sentenced to death. He carried his cross a long way and then up a hill to die for us.

Jesus warned his disciples that he would have to suffer, die, and then rise again. Along with that warning, he told them, "If any want to become my followers, let them deny themselves and take up their cross daily and follow me" (Luke 9:23). We can have many opportunities to deny ourselves and suffer in some small way for God and for others.

The Bible stories in this collection are meant to help you take up your cross daily. They will help you think about your life and how you can love others as Jesus loved us. He loved us so much that he died for us. The season of Lent is about taking up our crosses and denying ourselves in some small ways as we prepare to experience Jesus Christ's death and resurrection during Easter.

May God bless you and your families as you read these stories.

DUST TO DUST

Genesis 2-3

We begin each season of Lent with a day called Ash Wednesday. It is common to have our foreheads marked with ashes as a sign of our desire for mercy.

This is the story of God's punishment for Adam and Eve after they ate the forbidden fruit from the Tree of Knowledge. As you read this story, pay attention to the way God describes death to Adam.

When God made Adam in the Garden of Eden, he formed him out of the clay in the ground. He had big plans for Adam, but he also had one important rule: Do not eat the fruit from the Tree of Knowledge of Good and Evil.

"If you eat the fruit from that tree, you will die," God told him.

This command was given to Adam's wife, Eve, too. The Serpent, who is the devil, came and tempted

Eve. He persuaded her to eat the forbidden fruit. She gave some to her husband, Adam, who ate it as well.

They were immediately ashamed of disobeying God. They tried to hide from him, but God found them.

"You are banished from the garden. You will no longer eat the fruit from the Tree of Life," God told Adam. "Now you must work hard for your food. You must make bread for yourself to eat. Years from now, you will die and return to the ground. I made you out of the ground. You are dust, and to dust you shall return."

REFLECTION QUESTIONS

- *What punishment did God give to Adam for his sin?*
- *Why did God tell Adam he is dust and to dust he shall return?*
- *What does it feel like to do something wrong? How can you feel better after hurting or disobeying someone?*
- *Why do you think we look to Jesus' cross today as our new Tree of Life?*

THE TEMPTATION OF JESUS

Matthew 4:1–11; Mark 1:12–13; Luke 4:1–12

The season of Lent lasts for forty days and forty nights, the same amount of time Jesus spent in the desert after his baptism. One of the reasons we give something up during Lent is to train ourselves to resist temptation like Jesus did in this story.

As you read this story, pay attention to what Jesus says in response to the devil's temptations.

After Jesus was baptized, the Holy Spirit led him into a desert for forty days and forty nights. He fasted, which means he ate very little food. After the forty days were over, he was very hungry.

Then Satan came to tempt Jesus three times. Satan knew Jesus was hungry. "If you are the Son of God, turn stones into bread," he said.

Jesus resisted the temptation. He replied with a verse from Scripture, "One does not live by bread alone, but by every word that comes from the mouth of God."

Then the devil took him to the top of the Temple in Jerusalem. "If you are the Son of God, throw yourself down from this temple and God will command his angels to save you," said the devil.

Jesus resisted the temptation. Again he quoted Scripture, saying, "Do not put the Lord your God to the test."

Finally, the devil took him to a very high mountain where they could see all the kingdoms of the world. "All these I will give to you if you bow down and worship me," he said.

Jesus resisted this final temptation, too. "Away with you, Satan! Worship the Lord your God, and serve only him," he said, quoting Scripture once more.

Satan left him, and the angels did come to Jesus to serve him after all.

REFLECTION QUESTIONS

- *What does Jesus rely on in his defense against Satan?*
- *When and where can you read more of the Bible during Lent?*
- *Jesus was calm and strong against temptation even*

when he was hungry. How can you make yourself more patient and peaceful even when your stomach feels hungry?

NOAH AND THE FORTY-DAY FLOOD

Genesis 6-9

The number forty is very significant in the Old Testament. You probably remember the story about Noah's Ark. The people of the world were sinful. God called Noah to gather his family and two of every animal into his large boat (the ark) while he flooded the earth.

As you read this story, pay attention to how Noah knows God's flood is over after the forty days.

Noah loaded the last pair of animals onto his ark. The rain came down, and the water started to rise. The flood was so great that the water rose high above the mountains.

Only Noah, his family, and the many animals remained, floating above the water on the ark during the forty days of rain.

Then God finally sent a wind to settle the flood, and the waters died down. The ark settled on top of a mountain.

At the end of the forty days, Noah opened up a window and looked out over the earth. He sent out a dove to make sure the flood was over. The dove came back holding a branch from an olive tree, a sign of peace.

God made a promise to Noah never to flood the earth again. To show that promise, God sent a rainbow as another sign of peace. The rainbows that come after rain are a sign that God will not punish the whole earth again with a flood.

REFLECTION QUESTIONS

- *Noah had to wait forty days for the flood to end. Why is it so hard to be patient and wait?*
- *God was angry with the people of the earth. A dove came back to Noah with an olive branch as a sign of peace. When you are finished being angry with someone, what do you do to reunite with them?*

FORTY YEARS IN THE DESERT

Numbers 13–14

The season of Lent lasts for forty days, but the Israelites wandered the desert for forty years! God freed his people from slavery in Egypt and promised to give them the land of Canaan. Before they got there, however, God made them wander in the desert for forty years. This story explains why they had to suffer this punishment.

As you read this story, pay attention to the reason God punished the Israelites for specifically forty years.

The Israelites were freed from Egypt and eager to enter the land of Canaan. The only problem was that there were already people living in Canaan. God assured his people that he would be with them as they entered the new land.

God told Moses to send twelve spies into the land of Canaan, one spy for every tribe of Israel. The spies went out and traveled the land for forty days.

The spies came back and reported to Moses what they saw. The land was flowing with milk and honey. There were many places to grow food as farmers. But there were also many strong clans of people living there, and many of the spies were afraid of them.

Caleb and Joshua wanted to lead the Israelites to take the land right away. They were not afraid of the Canaanites. The other spies lied and said that they saw very tall and strong people, some of them the size of giants.

When the Israelites heard this, they became angry with Moses for leading them out of Egypt. They were afraid, too, and cursed God for bringing them there. They forgot God's promise that he would help them.

God was angry with the Israelites for their complaints. They did not trust in him, no matter how many signs and gifts he gave to them.

Moses prayed for forgiveness on behalf of the people. "Forgive the mistakes of this people, according to the greatness of your steadfast love," he prayed.

The Lord responded, "I do forgive, just as you have asked, but I will punish this generation of people for their lack of faith. You will wander in the desert for forty years, the same number as the number of days you spied out the land."

REFLECTION QUESTIONS

- *Why were the Israelites punished and sent into the desert for forty years?*
- *Have you or someone you know ever been like Caleb and Joshua, who had faith in God when everyone else was doubtful and afraid?*
- *Moses prayed for God to forgive his people. Who are the people in your life that pray for you?*

JONAH PREACHES IN NINEVEH

Jonah 3

Jonah was one of God's prophets. God wanted him to go to a foreign land called Nineveh, but Jonah didn't want to go. He tried to escape God's call by getting on a boat. God sent a storm, and Jonah was cast off the boat and swallowed by a whale. Most people know this part of the story, but they don't know what Jonah did after he got out of the belly of the whale.

This is the story of Jonah's prophecy in the land of Nineveh. As you read this story, pay attention to how the Ninevites respond to Jonah's message from God.

God was disappointed in the people of Nineveh. He sent his prophet Jonah into the city with a difficult message to proclaim. God was going to punish the people of Nineveh for their sins.

"In forty days, Nineveh shall be overthrown!" Jonah proclaimed. The city was very large. It took Jonah three days to walk through it, sharing the message from God.

When the people of Nineveh heard Jonah's words, they believed he was sent from God. The people who heard him declared a fast. They ate very little food. They put away their nice clothing and put on sackcloth instead. People wore sackcloth as a sign of humility and repentance for sin.

When the king of Nineveh heard Jonah's message, he also put away his royal robes and put on sackcloth. He made a proclamation in the city: "By the decree of the king: You shall not eat any food or drink any water. You shall put on sackcloth. You shall turn from your evil ways and from the violence in your hands. Who knows? God may change his mind. He may turn from his fierce anger with us so that we do not die."

God saw what the people of Nineveh did in response to Jonah's message. God changed his mind about the punishment he would bring upon them. Jonah's preaching was a success.

REFLECTION QUESTIONS

- *What did the people of Nineveh do when they heard God was angry with them and planning to punish them?*
- *What can you do during this season of Lent to show your sorrow for your sins?*

- *Instead of wearing sackcloth, how can you dress more simply during Lent as a sign of sorrow for your sins?*

THE PARABLE OF THE PERSISTENT WIDOW

Luke 18:1–8

The three most important ways for us to carry our crosses during Lent are prayer, fasting, and almsgiving. In this parable about prayer, Jesus encourages his disciples to be persistent. Too many times, we stop asking God for help because we give up or get distracted by other things in life.

As you read this parable, pay attention to what the widow does when the judge doesn't give an answer to her requests.

There once was a judge who did not fear God. He was mean to people and very disrespectful.

There was a widow who often came to the judge to ask for help. A widow is a woman whose husband has died. She was the victim of a crime, but the criminal was not punished.

"Grant me justice against my opponent," she said to the judge.

He refused her request.

She asked him again, but he still refused to help her.

The more she asked, however, the more he started to change his mind.

He thought to himself, "Though I have no fear of God and no respect for this widow, she won't stop bothering me. I will grant her justice so that she will stop coming to me for help."

Jesus explained this parable to his disciples saying, "Listen to what the unjust judge says. And will not God grant justice to the chosen ones who cry to him day and night? Will he delay long in helping them? I tell you, he will quickly grant justice to those who keep asking him for help."

REFLECTION QUESTIONS

- *Why did the judge grant the widow justice?*
- *Have you ever asked God for help without giving up, like the widow in the parable?*
- *What prayer request can you ask of God repeatedly, starting today?*

THE POOR WIDOW'S OFFERING

Mark 12:41–44; Luke 21:1–4

The three essential practices during Lent are prayer, fasting, and almsgiving. Almsgiving is the practice of giving money to the poor. In this story, Jesus points out the generosity of a poor widow as an example for us all to follow.

As you read this story, pay attention to the difference between what the rich people give and what the poor widow gives.

Jesus sat down with his disciples near the place where people came to donate money for the Temple. There was a box in which people placed their money. Jesus and the disciples watched as people came up to the box to put in their money.

First, many rich people in fancy clothing put in very large amounts of money. It was quite impressive, and these men walked away looking very proud of their generosity.

Then a woman walked up to the treasury box. She was dressed in worn-out clothing. She was a widow. Her husband had died, and she could not find work to make enough money to support herself. She was very poor.

From her pocket, she pulled out two pennies and put them in the treasury box.

Jesus said to his disciples, "This poor widow has put in more than all those who came before her. For all of them gave money that they didn't need for themselves. She gave everything she had. That was all she had to live on."

REFLECTION QUESTIONS

- *Why did Jesus praise the widow when she gave such a small amount of money compared to the rich people that came before her?*
- *What would be the hardest thing for you to give up for others? (Money? Clothes? Toys? Games? Devices?)*

THE PARABLE OF THE PHARISEE AND THE TAX COLLECTOR

Luke 18:9–14

Many people give things up during Lent as a form of fasting. Strictly speaking, fasting is refraining from food or certain types of food, but it can also refer to other forms of self-sacrifice.

Jesus fasted in the desert, after his baptism but before Satan came to tempt him. He told his followers who fast not to brag about it. He even shared a parable about someone who bragged about their prayer and fasting. As you read this story, pay attention to the differences between the way the two men speak to God in prayer.

Jesus told his disciples a parable about two men who went up to the temple to pray.

One of the men was a Pharisee. Pharisees were experts in God's Law. They were supposed to be holy and respectable people.

The other man was a tax collector. People gave money to tax collectors to give to their Roman rulers. People did not like tax collectors because they often took more money than they were supposed to collect. They kept this extra money for themselves.

The Pharisee stood alone in the temple and prayed, "God, I thank you that I am not like other people who break the law or even like that tax collector over there."

The Pharisee looked back at the tax collector and shook his head; then he continued his prayer, "I fast by not eating any food twice a week. I give ten percent of all the money I make to the Temple."

The tax collector was standing far from the Pharisee. His head was bowed. He would not even look up to heaven while he prayed. Instead, he beat his chest with his fist, praying, "God, be merciful to me, a sinner!"

Jesus explained this parable to his disciples. He said, "I tell you, the tax collector went home closer to God than the Pharisee. For all who pridefully exalt themselves will be humbled, but all who humble themselves will be exalted."

REFLECTION QUESTIONS

- *Have you kept your Lenten sacrifice between you*

and God, or have you tried to impress others with how holy you are?

- *How can you be more secretive about your sacrifices so that they are only between you and God?*

THE PRODIGAL SON'S PRAYER

Luke 15:11–24

Jesus told a story that we know as the Parable of the Prodigal Son. It is about a young son who wastes his share of his father's property. The father in the parable represents God our Father. The son in the story represents a person who sins but then seeks God's forgiveness.

As you read this story, pay attention to the words the son says in his apology to the father.

A man had two sons. Normally, a father would pass on his money and property to his sons after his death, but the younger son asked his father to give him his share early.

The younger son took all this money and traveled far away. He wasted it all away until he had nothing left. He was poor and hungry.

He went to a farmer and asked him for a job. The farmer sent him to take care of the pigs. Even the pigs ate better food than the young son was able to eat.

The son realized his mistake. He thought he could go home and ask his father to hire him as a servant. He planned to say these words:

"Father, I have sinned against heaven and against you. I no longer deserve to be called your son. Treat me as you would treat one of your hired workers."

When he returned home, his father saw him from a distance. The father ran to greet his son. He wrapped his arms around him. Then the young man said, "Father, I have sinned against heaven and against you. I no longer deserve to be called your son."

Instead, the father was filled with joy. He threw a big party to welcome his son home because his son was lost, but now he was back home.

REFLECTION QUESTIONS

- *How did the son seek the father's forgiveness in the parable?*
- *What similar prayer could we pray to God to seek forgiveness for our sins?*

JESUS ENTERS INTO JERUSALEM

Matthew 21:1-11; Mark 11:1-11; Luke 19:28-40

Palm Sunday is celebrated the week before Easter to remember the day that Jesus entered into Jerusalem, the city of his ancestor King David.

As you read this story, pay attention to the way the people greet Jesus and welcome him into the city.

Jesus travelled toward Jerusalem with his disciples. He sent two of them ahead of him to the village of Bethany to fetch a donkey for him. The disciples went and did as he told them.

The disciples put their cloaks over the donkey and Jesus rode it towards the city. A large crowd of people were gathered there to greet him. They took off their cloaks and laid them on the road. Others cut off branches from the palm trees nearby and spread them along the road.

Jesus rode along the cloaks and palms as the people sang:

"Hosanna to the Son of David! Blessed is he who comes in the name of the Lord! Hosanna in the highest!"

The people were amazed as they watched him ride along the road.

"Who is this?" some of them asked.

Others explained, "This is the prophet Jesus from Nazareth in Galilee."

REFLECTION QUESTIONS

- *Even though Jesus wasn't a king with an earthly kingdom, how did the people in Jerusalem show that they saw him as a king?*
- *What are some of the things you do "in the name of the Lord"? In other words, what do you do for others on behalf of God?*
- *If someone asked you who Jesus is, how would you respond?*

THE LAST SUPPER

Matthew 26:26–30; Mark 14:22–26; Luke 22:14–20

On the night before he died, Jesus celebrated the Passover feast with his disciples. There he instituted a new kind of feast for them to celebrate to remember him and what he did for them. This story tells the origin of the Eucharist and the celebration of communion we share at church.

As you read the story, pay attention to the way he describes his body (the bread) and his blood (the wine).

While they were eating the Passover feast, Jesus picked up a piece of bread and said a blessing. He broke it and gave it to his disciples, saying, "Take this and eat it, for this is my body, which will be given up for you."

Then he took the cup and gave thanks. He gave the cup to them to share and said, "Drink this, all of you, for this is my blood, the blood of the new covenant, which is poured out for many for the forgiveness of sins."

Then all gathered there sang a hymn together and went out to a mountain to pray.

REFLECTION QUESTIONS

- *What would happen to Jesus' body and blood after the Last Supper?*
- *Knowing what Jesus said about the bread and wine at the Last Supper, why is it important to celebrate communion?*

JESUS WASHES THE DISCIPLES' FEET

John 13:1–20

During the Last Supper, Jesus wanted to give his disciples one last gift before he died. He washed their feet.

As you read this story, pay attention to the way the disciples react to Jesus washing their feet.

After celebrating the Passover feast with his disciples, Jesus got up and took off his outer robe. He took a towel and wrapped it around his waist. He found a bowl and poured water into it.

Then he did something shocking. He went from disciple to disciple, kneeling down and washing each of their feet. He scrubbed their feet clean and dried them with his towel.

He came to Peter, who said, "Lord, are you really going to wash my feet?"

"Later you will understand," Jesus replied.

"You will never wash my feet," Peter said.

"Unless I wash your feet, you will have no share with me," Jesus said.

He finished washing their feet and put on his robe again. He returned to the table and said to them, "Do you know what I have done for you? You call me 'Teacher' and 'Lord,' and rightly so, for I am indeed. So if I, your Teacher and Lord, washed your feet, you also must wash one another's feet. I am setting an example for you to follow. As I have done, so you should also do."

REFLECTION QUESTIONS

- *How would you feel if you were one of the disciples and Jesus washed your feet?*
- *While you may not wash other people's feet, how can you humbly serve your friends, family, and other people you know?*

AGONY IN THE GARDEN

Matthew 26:36–46; Mark 14:32–42; Luke 22:39–46

The night before he died, Jesus went out to pray. He knew how difficult it was going to be to suffer and die on the cross.

He brought his disciples with him to pray in the garden, but their ability to pray was disappointing. As you read the story, pay attention to what Jesus says to the disciples when he finds them sleeping.

After sharing his Last Supper with his disciples, Jesus led them out to a garden called Gethsemane.

"Sit here while I go over there to pray," he told them. Then he asked Peter, James, and John to join him.

As they were walking, Jesus began to feel great sorrow and distress. "My soul is sorrowful even to the point of death," he said. "Remain here and keep watch with me."

Then Jesus went on a little farther to be alone. He fell down to the ground and prayed, "My Father, if it is possible, let this cup pass from me."

He knew he would have to die for the sins of God's people. It was going to be very, very difficult. He continued to pray, "But not as I will, but as you will."

He got up and returned to find Peter, James, and John asleep. He woke Peter up and said, "So you could not keep watch with me for one hour? Watch, and pray that you do not have to undergo such a challenge."

Peter was embarrassed but still very tired. "The spirit is willing, but the body is weak," Jesus told him.

Jesus went off again to be alone and again prayed that the cup would pass from him. Yet again, he said, "Your will be done!"

When he returned a second time, his disciples were sleeping again. Disappointed, Jesus went off to pray for a third time, saying the same prayer. Then, for the third time, his disciples fell asleep.

He returned and woke them up. "Are you still sleeping? Behold, the hour is at hand when I will be handed over to sinners."

REFLECTION QUESTIONS

- *How do you think the disciples felt after Jesus woke them up for the third time?*
- *What distracts you from staying focused during prayer?*
- *What do you want to pray about as we move closer to the celebration of Jesus' death and resurrection?*

BETRAYAL OF JUDAS

Matthew 26:14–16, 21–25, 47–56; Mark 14:10–11, 17–21, 43–52; Luke 22:3–6, 47–51; John 18:1–14

Jesus was betrayed by one his twelve closest disciples, Judas Iscariot. Judas had some disagreements with Jesus. Most of all, though, he was too worried about money.

As you read this story, pay attention to how Jesus reacts to the betrayal of Judas.

When Jesus and his disciples arrived in Jerusalem, Judas Iscariot went to the chief priests to betray Jesus. The priests were very pleased that he came to them. They wanted to arrest Jesus because they did not believe he was the Son of God.

"What will you give me if I betray him to you?" Judas asked.

"Thirty pieces of silver if you will lead us to Jesus," they said. Judas agreed and looked for his chance to turn Jesus in to them.

During their Last Supper, Jesus told the disciples that one of them would betray him. They were all shocked, even Judas. "Surely not I!" they all said in disbelief.

Jesus said to them, "It is the one who is dipping bread into the bowl with me. Woe to him. It would have been better for him not to have been born."

"Surely not I, Rabbi?" Judas asked again. He was dipping his bread in the bowl with Jesus.

"You have said so," replied Jesus.

After the supper, he took the disciples out to the garden of Gethsemane to pray. The disciples fell asleep, and Jesus went off by himself. Judas knew this was his chance to turn Jesus in to the chief priests. He went out and gathered a crowd of the priests, servants, and soldiers to lead them back to the garden. The men were armed with swords and clubs.

Along the way, he told the men, "The one I will kiss is the man. Arrest him."

When they arrived in the garden, Judas went up to Jesus and said, "Rabbi!" and kissed him.

Jesus replied, "Judas, do you betray me with a kiss? Friend, do what you are here to do."

Jesus did not resist them, but Peter tried to stop the guards. He took a sword and struck one of the high priest's slaves on the ear.

Jesus healed the man's ear and said, "Put the sword back into its place; for all who live by the sword will die by the sword. Do you think that I cannot ask the Father to send his angels to protect me? Let the scriptures be fulfilled. It must happen this way."

Then all the disciples deserted Jesus and ran away.

REFLECTION QUESTIONS

- *Why didn't Jesus stop Judas or resist being arrested?*
- *Greed was one of the reasons Judas betrayed Jesus. Are there any reasons you want money or possessions that might stand in the way of your relationship with God?*
- *Have you ever wanted to hit or fight someone when they did something against you? Why should you resist violence instead?*

THE DENIAL OF PETER

Matthew 26:31-35, 69-75; Mark 14:27-31, 66-72; Luke 22:31-34, 54-62; John 18:15-18, 25-27

After Jesus was arrested, his disciples fled and deserted him. Even his closest disciple, Peter, denied knowing Jesus for fear he would be arrested and killed, too.

As you read this story, pay attention to what Peter does afterward.

At the Last Supper, Jesus said to his disciples, "You will all become deserters because of me this night. But after I am raised up, I will go ahead of you to Galilee."

Peter said to him, "I will never desert you."

"Before the rooster crows in the morning, you will deny me three times."

"I would rather die than deny you, Jesus!" said Peter, and the other disciples agreed.

But when Jesus was arrested a short time later, they all fled in fear, despite what they had told Jesus.

Peter had escaped outside in a courtyard among many other people. A servant girl came to him and said, "You were with Jesus, weren't you?"

"I don't know what you are talking about," said Peter.

Another girl came up to him and said to the people around Peter, "This man was with Jesus of Nazareth!"

"I don't know the man," Peter promised.

Another person came up to Peter and said, "You must be one of Jesus' followers. You have the same accent as he does."

Peter cursed and said, "I do not know the man!"

Then he heard the sound of a rooster crowing. Peter remembered what Jesus had told him: "You will deny me three times."

He went out and cried bitterly.

REFLECTION QUESTIONS

- *Why did Peter deny Jesus?*
- *Why is it hard sometimes to talk about your faith in Jesus at school or outside of church?*

- *What do you say or do to show others you are a Christian?*

JESUS BEFORE PILATE

Luke 23:1-5, 13-15; John 18:28-38

Jesus was not directly killed by the leaders of his people. Instead, he was sentenced to death by Pontius Pilate, the Roman governor. Even though Pilate did not find him guilty, he sentenced him to death for fear of a revolt.

As you read this story, pay attention to the way Jesus responds to Pontius Pilate's questions.

The men who arrested Jesus brought him to Pontius Pilate's palace, where a crowd of people gathered outside.

"This man forbids us to pay taxes to the Roman emperor. He calls himself the Messiah, our king!" they said to the governor.

Pilate questioned Jesus, "Are you the king of the Jews?"

"Do you ask this on your own, or did others tell you about me?" Jesus said.

"I am not one of your people. Your chief priests handed you over to me. What did you do wrong?" Pilate asked him.

"My kingdom is not from this world. If it was, then my followers would be fighting to keep me from being handed over to death," Jesus said.

"So are you a king?" Pilate asked.

"You say so," Jesus replied.

Pilate turned to the chief priests and the crowds of people and said, "I find no proof against this man. I have not found this man guilty of any of your charges against him."

REFLECTION QUESTIONS

- *If Jesus' kingdom is not of this world, then where is his kingdom?*
- *How do you follow Jesus as your king and leader?*

JESUS AND BARABBAS

Mark 15:6–15; Luke 23:16–25; John 18:39–40

Pilate gave the crowds of people one last chance to free Jesus before he sentenced him to death. Jesus was innocent, but Barabbas was guilty of a crime. Pilate offered the crowd a choice to free Jesus or free a criminal.

As you read this story, pay attention to the way the people react to Pilate's offer to release Jesus.

Pilate did not see any proof that Jesus was guilty of the accusations the chief priests made against him. He would have set Jesus free, but he was afraid that the crowd of people gathered there would revolt. So he came up with a plan.

To the crowd of people and chief priests, he said, "I find no case against Jesus, but I have a custom to release someone for you at the Passover."

His guards brought forth another man. This man's name was Barabbas. Barabbas was in prison for revolting against the Roman Empire. He was accused of murder.

"Do you want me to release for you the king of the Jews?" Pilate asked the crowd.

"Not this man, but Barabbas!" they shouted.

Pilate wanted to release Jesus instead. "What evil has Jesus done? I find in him no reason to punish him with death."

But the people started shouting, "Crucify him! Crucify him!"

The shouts were loud, and their voices continued until Pilate finally gave the verdict. He released Barabbas to them. After having Jesus whipped, he handed him over to die on the cross.

REFLECTION QUESTIONS

- *If you were given a punishment for a crime you didn't commit, how would you react?*
- *In what ways do people still choose something or someone other than Jesus Christ?*

THE SOLDIERS MOCK JESUS

Matthew 27:27–31; Mark 15:16–20; John 19:1–3

Jesus was sentenced to death based on the accusation that he called himself the king of the Jews. Some of the Roman soldiers thought this was funny. This is the story of the way some Roman soldiers treated Jesus before his crucifixion.

As you read this story, notice how Jesus doesn't react or fight back.

Pilate sentenced Jesus to be crucified. The Roman soldiers who led him away thought they would have a little fun with him.

They clothed Jesus in a purple cloak. Purple was a color that the Roman emperor wore as a sign of his royalty. Then they found branches of thorns and wound them up into the shape of a crown. They placed this crown of thorns on Jesus' head.

The soldiers saluted Jesus, laughing as they said, "Hail, King of the Jews!"

Then they hit him in the face and spat on him.

They knelt down and mocked him as if he were a king. They laughed more as they stripped him of the purple cloak and put his own clothes back on.

Then they led him away to be crucified.

REFLECTION QUESTIONS

- *What does it feel like to be mocked and made fun of by others?*
- *Why do you think Jesus didn't object or argue with the soldiers?*
- *How does it make you feel to know that Jesus suffered all this mockery for you as your king?*

SIMON OF CYRENE CARRIES THE CROSS

Matthew 27:32; Mark 15:21; Luke 23:26

This is a very short story about a man who came to help Jesus carry the cross. Remember, Jesus said that to follow him, his disciples must "take up their cross daily" (Luke 9:23).

As you read this story, pay attention to why Simon of Cyrene helps Jesus carry the cross.

Pilate sentenced Jesus to death, and the Roman soldiers carried him off to be crucified.

It was a long way from the Roman governor's palace to the place where people were executed. They made Jesus carry the cross all by himself.

It was a difficult journey. Jesus fell many times. The Roman soldiers were frustrated.

A man named Simon was passing by. He was from a Greek city called Cyrene in Northern Africa. The soldiers seized Simon and placed the cross on his shoulders to carry for Jesus.

Jesus walked ahead without the burden of the cross for just a little way while Simon followed behind. Then, when Simon could walk no farther, they placed the cross back on Jesus' shoulders.

Simon watched as Jesus was led off to be crucified.

Simon had two sons, Alexander and Rufus. They became followers of Christ. Rufus became a friend and companion to Paul in the years after Jesus' death.

REFLECTION QUESTIONS

- *Why did Simon of Cyrene carry the cross?*
- *What unexpected chances have you had to carry a cross for Jesus?*

THE INRI SIGN

John 19:19–22

If you look closely at a crucifix, you will see the letters INRI on a paper nailed to the cross above the head of Jesus. These letters are for the Latin words "Iesus Nazarenus Rex Iudaeorum," which means, "Jesus of Nazareth, King of the Jews." This is the story of why those words were written on the cross.

As you read this story, pay attention to the reasons people objected to the sign above Jesus' head.

When the Roman governor, Pilate, asked Jesus if he was the king of the Jews, Jesus said, "You say so."

So when he sent him off to be crucified, Pilate had someone make a sign in large letters reading, "Jesus of Nazareth, the King of the Jews." He had them nail this sign to the top of Jesus' cross.

The chief priests, who wanted to kill Jesus for acting like the Messiah, objected to Pilate. "Do not write,

'The King of the Jews,'" they told him. "Instead write, 'This man said: I am King of the Jews.'"

"What I have written I have written," Pilate answered them.

REFLECTION QUESTIONS

- *If Jesus really was the king of the Jews, why would the chief priests and others be embarrassed by the sign?*
- *In what ways do people know you are a follower of the King of Kings, Jesus of Nazareth?*

CRIMINALS ON THE CROSS

Luke 23:32, 39–40

Jesus was not crucified alone. There were criminals there with him who were also sentenced to death. This is the story of a conversation Jesus had with the two other men who were crucified by his side.

As you read this story, pay attention to what Jesus promises to the criminal who stands up for him.

The soldiers nailed Jesus' hands and feet to the cross and raised it high. Two criminals were also nailed to crosses on his right and his left.

One of the criminals said, "Are you not the Messiah? Save yourself and us!"

But the other criminal scolded the man. "Do you not fear God? You are condemned to death just like us, but you and I are getting what we deserve. This man has done nothing wrong."

He looked to Jesus and said, "Jesus, remember me when you come into your kingdom."

Jesus replied, "Today you will be with me in Paradise."

REFLECTION QUESTIONS

- *What is the Paradise that Jesus promises to the criminal who spoke up for him?*
- *When have you felt like either one of the criminals who were crucified with Jesus?*

JOHN AND MARY AT THE CROSS

John 19:25–27

While most of the disciples deserted Jesus, some of the women who were closest to him stayed, including his mother. The apostle John was also there at the cross, and Jesus took the opportunity to speak to him and his mother.

As you read this story, pay attention to the new relationship between Mary and the disciple.

After Jesus was arrested, almost all of his disciples deserted him, but Jesus was not completely alone on the cross.

Three Marys stood near the cross: his mother Mary; his aunt Mary, the wife of Clopas; and a follower named Mary Magdalene. The apostle John was also there.

Just before he took his last breath, Jesus saw his mother and his disciple John standing beside her.

He said to his mother, "Woman, here is your son."

Then he looked to his disciple and said, "Here is your mother."

John took Jesus' mother Mary into his home from that day forward, long after Jesus died and rose again.

REFLECTION QUESTIONS

- *What do you think Jesus' mother Mary was feeling as she stood near the cross?*
- *If you were the apostle John, how would you treat Jesus' mother in the days and years that followed?*

LAST WORDS OF CHRIST

Matthew 27:45–54; Mark 15:33–39; Luke 23:44–48; John 19:28–30

People often tell stories of the last words spoken by famous people or close family members or friends. This is the story of the last words Jesus spoke before he died.

As you read this story, pay attention to what the Roman centurion says after Jesus dies.

Jesus had been hanging on the cross for hours when darkness started to come over the land. Then, at three o'clock in the afternoon, Jesus cried out, *"Eloi, Eloi, lema sabachthani?"*

This means, "My God, my God, why have you forsaken me?" Jesus was quoting the opening verse of Psalm 22 from Scripture.

The people there didn't understand. They thought he said something else. "Listen, he is calling for the prophet Elijah," someone said.

Some people there ran to grab a stick and a sponge. They soaked the sponge in wine and gave it to Jesus to drink.

"Wait, let us see if Elijah will come to take him down," said another person standing there.

"It is finished," Jesus said. He bowed his head and took his last breath.

At that moment, an earthquake shook the land. Elsewhere, the curtain in the Temple split in two.

A Roman centurion was there keeping watch over Jesus and the cross. When he saw that Jesus was dead and felt the earthquake, he said in fear, "Certainly, this man was innocent. Truly, he was the Son of God!"

REFLECTION QUESTIONS

- *Why would God send his only son to die even though he was innocent? How does this sacrifice for you make you feel?*
- *If you could plan your last words before you die, what would they be?*

JESUS' SIDE IS PIERCED

John 19:31-37

Art and sculptures of Jesus' body on the cross show the wounds on his hands, feet, and side. This is the story of why Jesus' side was cut during his crucifixion.

As you read this story, pay attention to why Jesus' side was pierced with a spear.

After a long and difficult passion, Jesus died on the cross. The holy sabbath day was approaching, and this was the day of the week when the Jews rested. So the Jews asked the Roman governor, Pilate, to remove the bodies from the cross.

He ordered the soldiers to break the legs of the men being crucified to make sure they would all be dead before sundown. So the soldiers went down the line of crosses, breaking the legs of the men hanging on each one.

But when they came to Jesus, the soldiers could see he was already dead. So one of them took his spear and cut Jesus on his side to be sure. Blood and water came out.

A Christian eyewitness was there to see all this.

The wound on Jesus' side was later the proof that the apostle Thomas later needed to believe that the risen Jesus who appeared to him was really the Lord.

REFLECTION QUESTIONS

- *Why was Jesus' side pierced on the cross?*
- *How could we know about all these events during Jesus' death on the cross?*
- *What helps you believe in Jesus?*

JESUS BURIED IN A TOMB

John 19:38-42

After suffering much and dying on the cross, Jesus body was taken down and buried. This is the story of his burial after death.

As you read this story, pay attention to why Pilate gave the body to Jesus' followers.

On the evening that Jesus died, the Jews were preparing for the sabbath day of rest. A man named Joseph from a nearby city called Arimathea was there. He was rich and a member of the council. He was secretly a disciple of Jesus and looked for the coming of the Kingdom of God.

After Jesus died, Joseph boldly went to Pilate and asked for the body of Jesus. Pilate checked with one of his soldiers to make sure Jesus was dead. When he learned that Jesus had been dead for some time, he granted Joseph permission to take the body.

The soldiers took down the body, and Joseph wrapped it in a linen cloth, according to their burial customs. He placed the body in a stone tomb for burial. He rolled a very heavy stone across the door of the tomb.

Jesus' mother Mary and Mary Magdalene were there to see where Jesus was buried.

REFLECTION QUESTIONS

- *Why do you think Pilate wanted to be sure Jesus was dead before giving the body to Joseph of Arimathea?*
- *Joseph had courage when he approached the Roman governor. How can you show courage in your faith in Jesus?*

EASTER SUNDAY MORNING

Matthew 28:1–10; Mark 16:1–7; Luke 24:1–10; John 20:1–10

Here is a fitting end to this collection of stories for the season of Lent. The story of Jesus' death does not end in the tomb. He died and rose again so that we might also die and rise with him in the Kingdom of Heaven.

As you read this story, pay attention to what the women do when they see the empty tomb.

On Sunday morning, the first day of the week, Mary Magdalene, Mary the mother of the apostles James and John, and a woman named Joanna went to Jesus' tomb. They brought with them spices to anoint his body.

Along the way, Mary Magdalene asked the others, "Who will roll back the stone for us from the entrance of our Lord's tomb?"

The others did not know the answer. Still they went on their way.

As they arrived at the tomb, the sun was rising. They were astonished to see that the very large stone covering the entrance had already been rolled away.

They ran to the tomb and looked inside. The body of Jesus was gone!

Then two angels wearing dazzling clothing appeared. The women were terrified. They covered their faces and looked to the ground.

"Why do you look for the living among the dead?" the angels said to them. "You seek Jesus of Nazareth. He is not here. He has been raised!"

The women's eyes filled with tears. They suddenly remembered that Jesus said the Son of Man would die and rise again on the third day.

They left the tomb and went to announce what they had seen to the other disciples.

REFLECTION QUESTIONS

- *What proof did the women have that Jesus had risen from the dead?*
- *How can you announce to others the great gift of Jesus' death and resurrection?*

ABOUT BIBLE BREAKS

The Bible Breaks stories for kids help families and faith formation groups set aside a few minutes during the day to read and reflect on the Word of God. Each short and simple story is written to help teach children the most important lessons of the Christian life from Sacred Scripture.

Learn more at jareddees.com/biblebreaks

ALSO BY JARED DEES

Jared Dees is the author of numerous books, including another short story collection titled *Beatitales: 80 Fables about the Beatitudes for Children*.

Download a collection of these stories at jareddees.com/beatitales.

BOOKS BY JARED DEES

31 Days to Becoming a Better Religious Educator

To Heal, Proclaim, and Teach

Praying the Angelus

Christ in the Classroom

Beatitales

Tales of the Ten Commandments

Do Not Be Afraid

Take and Eat

Pray without Ceasing

Prepare the Way

ABOUT THE AUTHOR

Jared Dees is the creator of *TheReligionTeacher.com*, a popular website that provides practical resources and teaching strategies to religious educators. A respected graduate of the Alliance for Catholic Education (ACE) program at the University of Notre Dame, Dees holds master's degrees in education and theology, both from Notre Dame. He frequently gives keynotes and leads workshops at conferences, church events, and school in-services throughout the year on a variety of topics. He lives near South Bend, Indiana, with his wife and four daughters.

Learn more about Jared's books, speaking events, and other projects at jareddees.com.

amazon.com/author/jareddees

facebook.com/jareddeesauthor

instagram.com/jareddees

twitter.com/jareddees

youtube.com/thereligionteacher